MY BOOK

one

My picture
or drawing

MY ENGLISH ZONE

Published by UnilX Education

books@unilxeducation.com
USA +1 619 798 6274
MEX +52 6631030487

MyEnglishGameZone®, 2021 ©UnilX LLC, 2021

First Published 2021

Author: Patricia Armida Ávila Delfín
Editor: Sandra Rojas
Main Characters: My English Game Zone®
Cover and Complimentary Graphics: UnilX, Innovalingua Design Team and Freepik.com
Illustration, Design and Animation Leader: Rafael Orellana
Editorial Design: UNIGRÁPHICA, UnilX editorial team, Rafael Orellana

PROGRAM SYNOPSIS

The fundamental objective of **My English Zone The Book** is learning to communicate through interaction in the target language. The Theory of Language learning tells us that "language is a tool for communication and that students learn a language by using it to communicate."

You will find that **My English Zone The Book** is a series based on guided everyday communicative interaction. E.g. when students are faced with real life dialogs to find out the schedule of the week's exams or to describe a classmate by his/her physical appearance, among many other authentic situations. Guided dialogs provide opportunities for language learners to interact with each other or with native speakers while feeling comfortable doing so.

This series also acknowledges the role of grammar as that of great importance for our learners to reach higher levels of proficiency and introduces the basic structures from the start of the program.

My English Zone The Book also makes extensive use of authentic texts like: songs, jokes, rhymes, tongue twisters and popular children's stories. They will enrich the knowledge of culture through language.

As you can see, **My English Zone The Book** has a solid base on the most important methodologies necessary to enhance the learning of the second language in a dynamic and fun way.

Patricia Avila Delfin

SERIES FEATURES

- Each book with 15 units.
- Each unit has five lessons:

Book number	CEFR
1	Pre-A1
2	Pre-A1
3	A1.1
4	A1.2
5	A2.1
6	A2.1
7	A2.2
8	A2.2
9	B1.1
10	B1.2
11	B1.3
12	B1+

Lesson 1: Vocabulary

In this first lesson the vocabulary that will be used during the rest of the unit will be presented through clear images that represent each word.

Lesson 2: Dialogs

The dialogs will recap the vocabulary items from lesson one and use them in everyday real situations.

Lesson 3: Reading

The reading texts will go from original stories that take the ideas of the dialogs and complete them in a text to popular stories from children's literature.

Lesson 4: Writing

Prompted writing is used in the lower levels. It encourages students to use their imagination to come up with new and creative ideas for the text. In the higher levels, students will be asked to arrange the paragraphs or the missing sentences to complete the stories they read before.

Lesson 5: Language in Use

The last part of each unit, recaps the grammar structures seen, through the presentation of language in use of the four lessons before it. There are activities that will evaluate the knowledge acquired.

METHODOLOGIES

Vocabulary Learning

Vocabulary learning is central to language acquisition.

Specialists emphasize the need for a systematic and principled approach of vocabulary by the teacher and the learner. Teaching techniques and activities state that new words should not be learned by simple rote memorization.

It is important that new vocabulary items be presented in contexts rich enough to provide clues to meaning and that students be given multiple exposure to items they should learn.

Communicative Language Learning

Learning to communicate through interaction in the target language is the principal characteristic of the Communicative Language Teaching approach.

The The*ory of Language Learning states that:*
• *Langu*age is a tool for communication
• Students learn a language by using it to communicate

Integrated Skills Approach

The four basic skills in language teaching are: listening, speaking, reading , writing .

When we acquire a second language in a natural way the skills appear in that same order.

But why should we integrate the four skills when teaching the second language? If we are focused on teaching a realistic communication competence, the four skills must be developed in an integrated way .

Integrating the skills allows us to use more variety in the lessons because the range of activities will be ampler.

Spiral Learning

Learning should work like a game in a spiral, that gets a child interested while repeating and gradually increasing difficulty. It also gives students challenging activities and at the same time adds new skills.

The steps to achieve Spiral Learning are:
•   Introduce new language. Move forward.
•   Recap the important language learned so far.
•   Add more language.
•   Recap selected language: recent and earlier.
•   Repeat the process.

Topic Based Approach

Topic based approach is student-centered. It helps with students' attention span.
It will hold students' interest from the start to the end of the lesson.

CONTENTS MAP

5

MY PLATFORM ACCESS

URL: _____

User name: _____

Password: _____

MY ENGLISH ZONE

Ask your teacher or parents if you have a platform access.

Practice the following dialogs

Good morning my name is Miss Patty.
What's your name?
-Hello! My name is Sandy

Hi! My name is Tony.
What's Your name?
-Good morning!
-My name is Lucy.

Hello! My name is Andy.
What's your name?
-Hello! My name is…
               (your name)

Now you!

Ask your classmate's name.
Good morning!
My name is _____
WHAT'S YOUR NAME?

_____

Match the names to your new friends

Andy

Lucy

Sandy

Tony

Miss Paty

Learn the alphabet

A a	✈	G g	🦒
B b	🏀	H h	🐎
C c	🐱	I i	🧊
D d	🐬	J j	🫙
E e	🦅	K k	👑
F f	🌸	L l	🦁

M m	👩	T t	🐯
N n	👩‍⚕️	U u	🦄
O o	🍊	V v	🧛
P p	✏️	W w	🐺
Q q	👸	X x	🎼
R r	🌹	Y y	🧶
S s	☀️	Z z	🦓

Match the letter with its picture

Aa Bb Cc Dd Ee Ff

Gg Hh Ii Jj Kk Ll

Mm Nn Oo Pp Qq Rr Ss

Tt Uu Vv Ww Xx Yy Zz

Trace each capital and small letter. Say it aloud.

Aa	A a	A a
Bb	B b	B b
Cc	C c	C c
Dd	D d	D d
Ee	E e	E e
Ff	F f	F f

Gg	G g	G g
Hh	H h	H h
Ii	I i	I i
Jj	J j	J j
Kk	K k	K k
Ll	L l	L l

Mm	M m	M m
Nn	N n	N n
Oo	O o	O o
Pp	P p	P p
Qq	Q q	Q q
Rr	R r	R r
Ss	S s	S s

Tt	T t	T t
Uu	U u	U u
Vv	V v	V v
Ww	W w	W w
Xx	X x	X x
Yy	Y y	Y y
Zz	Z z	Z z

Sing the alphabet song!

Aa Bb Cc Dd

Ee Ff Gg Hh

Ii Jj Kk Ll

Mm Nn Oo Pp

Qq Rr Ss Tt

Uu Vv Ww Xx

Yy Zz

How well did you do in this unit?

Write the CAN DO statement and assess yourself:

I can...

Learn the numbers

1
one

6
six

2
two

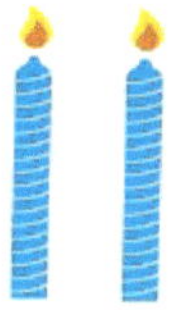

7
seven

3
three

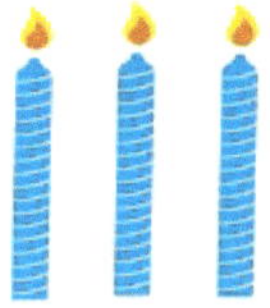

8
eight

4
four

9
nine

5
five

10
ten

Practice the dialogs

Good morning! What's your name?
-Good morning! My name is Sandy.
How old are you Sandy?
-I am six years old.

Good morning! What's your name?
-Good morning! My name is Lucy.
How old are you Lucy?
-I am six years old.

Hello! What's your name?
-Hello! My name is Andy.
How old are you Andy?
-I am seven years old.

Hello! What's your name?
-Hello! My name is Tony.
How old are you Tony?
-I am seven years old.

Now you!

Good morning! What's your name?
Good morning! My name is _____.
How old are you _____?
I am _____ years old.

14

Welcome to school

Miss Patty welcomes us
to school every day.
Miss Patty asks: How old are you?
I am 6 years old, answers Sandy.
I am 7 years old, answers Tony.
I am 6 years old, answers Lucy.
I am 7 years old, answers Andy.
We are all in first grade.
I love school!

Complete the sentences

1. Sandy is _____ years old.
   four   five   six

2. Tony is _____ years old.
   seven   six   three

3. Lucy is _____ years old.
   two   three   six

4. Andy is _____ years old.
   one   seven   eight

5. You are _____ years old.
   five   six   seven

Complete the reading with the words from the box below

Welcome to school

Miss Patty welcomes us to school every day.
Miss Patty asks: How old are you?
I am _____ years old, answers Sandy.
I am _____ years old, answers Tony.
I am _____ years old, answers Lucy.
I am _____ years old, answers Andy.
I am _____ years old, I answer.
We are all in first grade.
I love school!

one • two • three • four • five • six

seven • eight • nine • ten

Write the words. Say them aloud.

1	one	5	five	9	nine
2	two	6	six	10	ten
3	three	7	seven		
4	four	8	eight		

Match the numbers with their name

eight	1
five	2
four	3
nine	4
one	5
seven	6
six	7
ten	8
three	9
two	10

Complete the numbers

e __ gh __

f _ v __

f __ __ r

ni __ __

__ n __

__ __ ven

si __

te __

thr __ __

t __ o

Sing the song

This old man

This old man, he played one,
He played knick-knack on my thumb;
** With a knick-knack paddywhack,
Give a dog a bone,
This old man came rolling home.
This old man, he played two,
He played knick-knack on my shoe;
** (repeat)
This old man, he played three,
He played knick-knack on my knee;
** (repeat)
This old man, he played four,
He played knick-knack on my door;
** (repeat)
This old man, he played five,
He played knick-knack on my hive;
** (repeat)

This old man, he played six,
He played knick-knack on my sticks;
** (repeat)
This old man, he played seven,
He played knick-knack up in Heaven;
** (repeat)
This old man, he played eight,
He played knick-knack on my gate;
** (repeat)
This old man, he played nine,
He played knick-knack on my spine;
** (repeat)
This old man, he played ten,
He played knick-knack once again;
** (repeat)

How well did you do in this unit?

Write the CAN DO statement and assess yourself:

I can...

Learn the classroom language

color

Open your book!

write

point

Sit down, please!

Be quiet, please!

Close your book!

Stand up, please!

listen

repeat

Practice the dialogs

Lucy, open your book please!
-Yes, Miss Patty.
Thank you.

Sandy, close your book please!
-Yes, Miss Patty.
Thank you

Tony, be quiet please!
-Yes, Miss Patty
Thank you.

Andy, stand up please!
-Yes, Miss Patty.
Thank you.

Write the homework!
-Yes, Miss Patty
Thank you.

Repeat after me!
-Yes, Miss Patty
Thank you.

Color the picture!
-Yes, Miss Patty.
Thank you.

Now you!

You: _____
Your classmate: _____
You: _____
Your classmate: _____

Our English class

My friends and I are very happy in our English class.
We learn new words every day like:
listen, repeat, write, color and point.
We also learn new expressions like:
stand up, sit down, open your book and be quiet.
I am very happy in my English class
because I learn new things every day!
Thank you teacher!

Answer the questions

1. What words do you learn at school?
   a) one, two, three   b) listen, repeat, write
2. What expressions do you learn in your English class?
   a) stand up, sit down   b) five, six, seven
3. How do you feel in English class?
   a) angry   b) happy
4. What do you learn in class every day?
   a) new things   b) nothing

Match the words with the correct image

Write the words.
Say them aloud.

listen

repeat

write

color

point

stand up

sit down

be quiet

listen

repeat

write

color

point

stand up

sit down

be quiet

open

close

Complete the words. Match them with their image.

li___ te___

r___p___a___

wr___t___

c___l___r

poi___t

s___a___d up

sit ___o___n

be ___ui___t

ope___

___l___se

Say the rhyme:
Mary Had a Little Lamb

Mary had a little lamb,
It's fleece was white as snow;
And everywhere that Mary went,
The lamb was sure to go.

If followed her to school one day,
Which was against the rule;
It made the children laugh and play,
To see a lamb at school.

How well did you do in this unit?

_____

Write the CAN DO statement and assess yourself:

I can...

_____

_____

_____

_____

_____

Learn the days of the week and the words for the weather

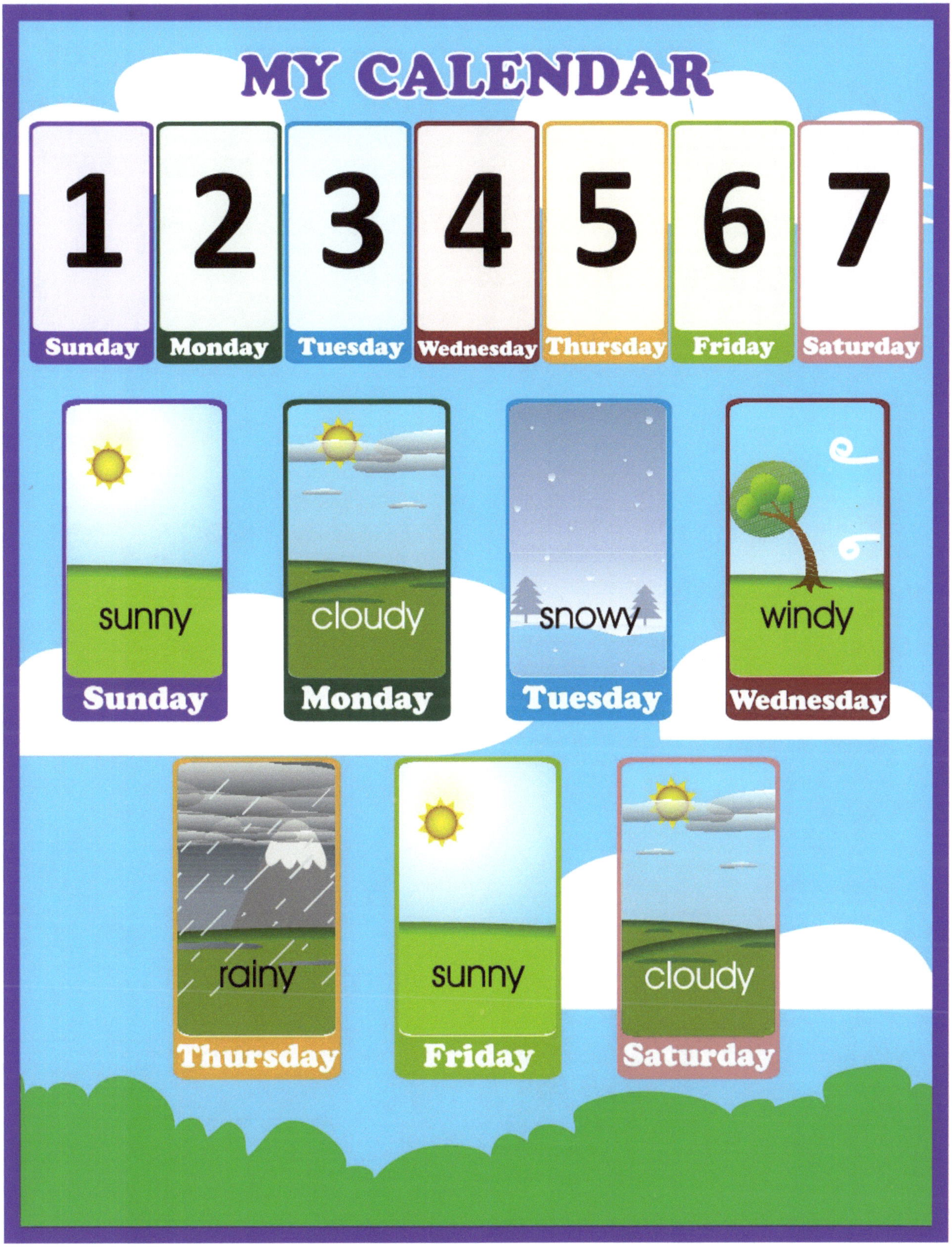

MY CALENDAR

1	2	3	4	5	6	7
Sunday	Monday	Tuesday	Wednesday	Thursday	Friday	Saturday

sunny
Sunday

cloudy
Monday

snowy
Tuesday

windy
Wednesday

rainy
Thursday

sunny
Friday

cloudy
Saturday

What day is today?

-Today is Monday.

How is the weather?

-It is cloudy.

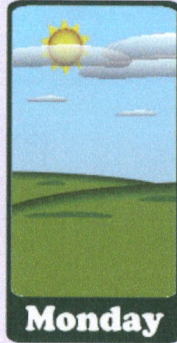

What day is today?

-Today is Thursday.

How is the weather?

-It is rainy.

What day is today?

-Today is Tuesday.

How is the weather?

-It is snowy.

What day is today?

-Today is Friday.

How is the weather?

-It is sunny.

What day is today?

-Today is Wednesday.

How is the weather?

-It is windy.

Now you!

What day is today?
Today is _____.
How is the weather?
It is _____.

Beautiful weather

This week we see beautiful weather on our calendar every day.

On Sunday, it is sunny.

On Monday, it is cloudy.

On Tuesday, it is snowy.

On Wednesday, it is windy.

On Thursday, it is rainy.

Our calendar looks beautiful!

sunny — Sunday
cloudy — Monday
snowy — Tuesday
windy — Wednesday
rainy — Thursday

Answer the questions

How is the weather on Sunday?
a) sunny b) snowy c) cloudy

How is the weather on Monday?
a) snowy b) cloudy c) windy

How is the weather on Tuesday?
a) rainy   b) cloudy c) snowy

How is the weather on Wednesday?
a) sunny b) windy   c) rainy

Answer the questions with the correct days

1. What day is it sunny?
_____.

2. What day is it cloudy?
_____.

3. What day is it rainy?
_____.

4. What day is it snowy?
_____.

Complete the reading with words from the box below. You may write them in any order you wish.

Beautiful weather

This week every day we see beautiful weather on our c a l e n d a r .

On _____ , it is _____ .

On _____ , it is _____ .

On _____ , it is _____ .

Our calendar looks beautiful!

Monday • Tuesday • Wednesday • Thursday • Friday
sunny • cloudy • windy • rainy • snowy

Write the words. Say them aloud.

Sunday	Thursday	windy
Monday	Friday	rainy
Tuesday	sunny	snowy
Wednesday	cloudy	

We use **IS** for the singular form of the verb to **BE**.

The days of the week need a capital letter at the beginning of the word.

We must put a question mark at the end of the question. (?)

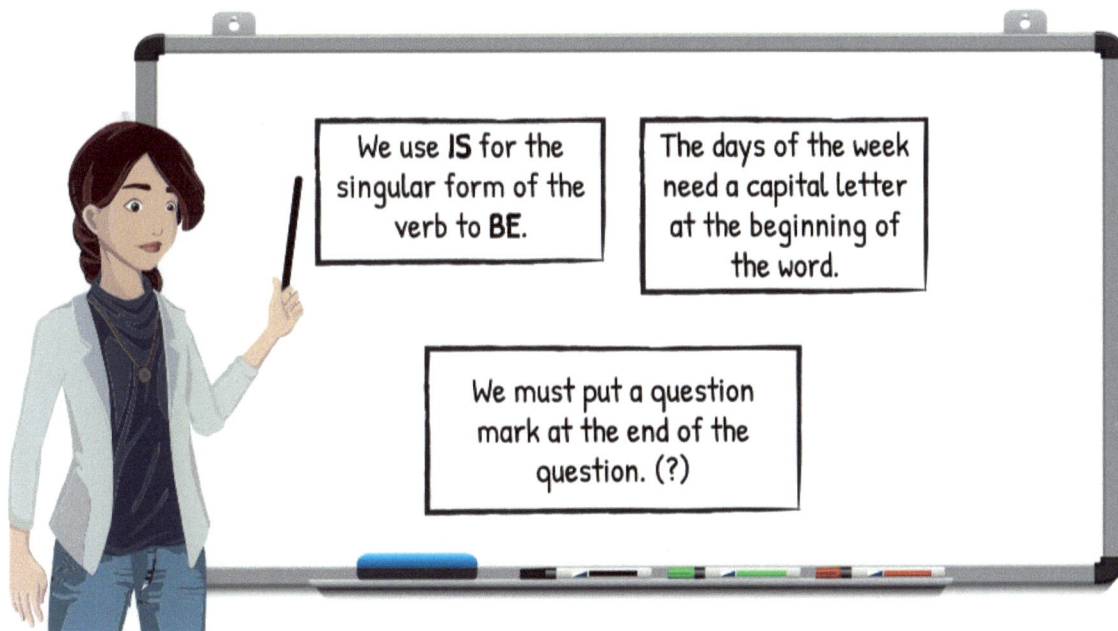

Choose the correct letter

a) _____ onday
   M   m

b) _____ uesday
   t   T

c) _____ ednesday
   W   w

d) _____ unday
   s   S

e) _____ riday
   F   f

Complete the sentences

1. Today _____ _____ onday.
          is   M   m

2. It _____ _____ unny.
      S   s   is

3. What day _____ today _____
            ?   is   T

4. Today _____ _____ riday.
          F   f   is

5. It _____ _____ indy.
      W   is   w

6. How _____ the weather _____
        W   ?   is

29

How well did you do in this unit?

Write the CAN DO statement and assess yourself:

I can...

Learn the places in your school

library

computer room

restroom

school yard

cafeteria

office

music room

theater

classroom

Practice the dialogs

What is this?
-This is the classroom.

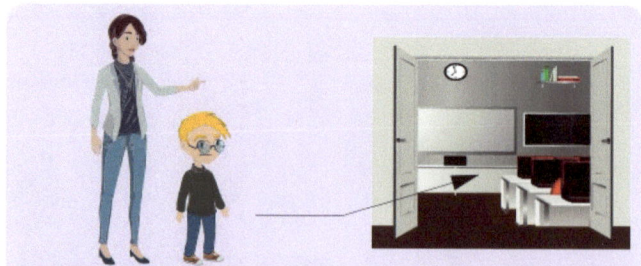

What is that?
-That is the computer room.

What is this?
-This is the music room.

What is that?
-That is the restroom.

What is this?
-This is the cafeteria.

What is that?
-That is the library.

What is this?
-This is the office.

Now you!

What is that/this?
-That/this is the _____.

Welcome to school

This is our beautiful school:
This is the classroom and
that is the restroom.
This is the music room and
That is the library.
This is the cafeteria and
that is the theater.
This is the computer room and
that is the school yard.
This is the office.
Our school is beautiful, I love our school!

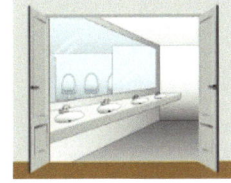

Choose the correct answer

What is this?
- This is the computer room
- This is the classroom.
- This is the restroom.

What is that?
- That is the library.
- That is the music room.
- That is the classroom.

What is this?
- This is the office.
- This is the school yard.
- This is the restroom.

Complete the reading with the words from the box below

This is our beautiful school:

This is the _____ and that is the _____.

This is the _____ and that is the _____.

This is the _____ and that is the _____.

This is the _____ and that is the _____.

This is the _____.

Our school is beautiful, I love our school!

restroom • computer room • office • cafeteria
school yard • music room • classroom • theater • library

Write the words. Say them aloud.

restroom   music room

computer room   classroom

office   theater

cafeteria   library

school yard

Let's play **at school!**
5.5
Language in use

DEMONSTRATIVE PRONOUNS

A demonstrative pronoun points out a particular person, place, or thing.

This point out nouns that are near the person speaking.

That point out things that are far from the person speaking.

This and **that** are singular pronouns

Choose the correct picture

That is the restroom.

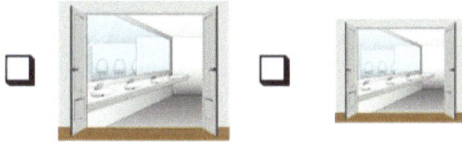

□   □

This is the office.

□   □

That is the cafeteria.

□   □

This is the music room.

□   □

Write the correct demonstrative pronoun

_____   this   that

_____   this   that

_____   this   that

_____   this   that

_____   this   that

How well did you do in this unit?

Write the CAN DO statement and assess yourself:

I can...

Learn the objects in your classroom

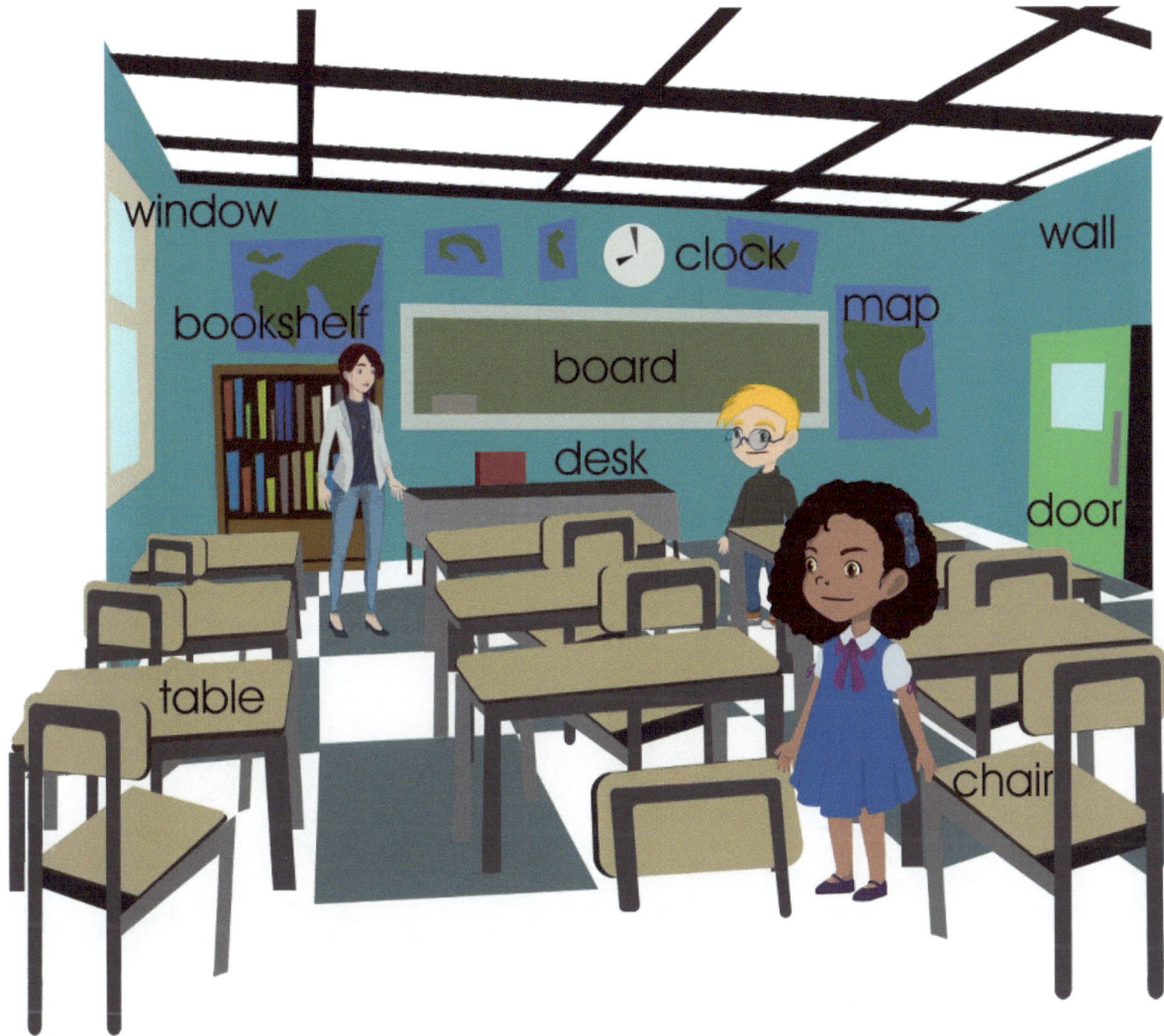

window
wall
bookshelf
clock
map
board
desk
door
table
chair

Practice the dialogs

Is this the desk?
-Yes, that is the desk.

Is this the bookshelf?
-Yes, that is the bookshelf.

Is this the book?
-Yes, that is the book.

Is this the board?
-Yes, that is the board.

Now you!

Is this a _____?
Yes, that is a _____.

Welcome to our classroom

Welcome to our classroom!!

Miss Patty welcomes us
to our classroom,
she shows us many things.

Look! This is the board and that is the bookshelf.
This is the chair and that is the clock.
This is the desk and that is the door.
That is the map and this is the table.
That is the wall and this is the window.
I love our classroom!

Choose the correct sentence

What is this?
a) This is the bookshelf
b) This is the board

What is that?
a) That is the bookshelf
b) That is the board

What is this?
a) This is the desk
b) This is the chair

Choose the correct picture.

Is this the chair ?
- Yes, that is the chair.
❑ ❑ ❑

Is this the board ?
- Yes, that is the board.
❑ ❑ ❑

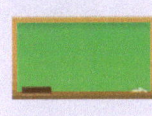

Is this the desk ?
- Yes, that is the desk.
❑ ❑ ❑

Complete the reading with the words from the box below

Welcome to our classroom

Miss Patty welcomes us to our classroom,
she shows us many things.

Look! This is the _____ and that is the _____.

This is the _____ and that is the _____.

This is the _____ and that is the _____.

That is the _____ and this is the _____.

That is the _____ and this is the _____.

I love our classroom!

board • bookshelf • chair • clock • desk • door
map • table • wall • window

Write the words. Say them aloud.

board	desk	table
chair	door	wall
clock	map	window

To make a question with the verb BE the subject and the verb change positions.

Affirmative: This is a map.

Interrogative: Is this a map?

To give a short affirmative answer we always use:
Yes, (comma) **it is.** (period)
We do not use a contracted form for the short answer.
Yes, it's.

Change the sentences into questions

1. This is the bookshelf.
_____?

2. This is the board.
_____?

3. This is the desk.
_____?

4. This is the chair.
_____?

5. This is the map.
_____?

Choose the correct short answer

Is this the chair?
a) Yes this is. b) Yes, it is. c) Yes it is

Is this the wall?
a) Yes, it is. b) Yes, is it? c) Yes this is.

Is this the clock?
a) Yes, it's.   b) Yes, it is.   c) Yes is it.

Is this the bookshelf?
a) Yes, it's b) Yes, this is. c) Yes, it is.

Is this the table?
a) Yes, it is. b) Yes, it's. c) Yes, is this.

How well did you do in this unit?

_____

Write the CAN DO statement and assess yourself:

I can...

Learn the school objects in your backpack

scissors

book

pencil

notebook

eraser

sharpener

ruler

crayon

marker

pen

Practice the dialogs

Where is the pen?
- It is on the chair.

Where is the pencil?
- It is under the table.

Where is the crayon?
- It is in the school bag.

Where is the book?
- It is on the bookshelf.

Where is the sharpener?
- It is under the chair.

Now you!

Where is the_____?
It is on the_____.

This is my school bag

My school bag is beautiful.
The pencil is in the bag.
The pen is in the bag too.
The crayon is in the bag and
the notebook is also in the bag.
Oops! Where is the ruler?
-It is on the desk.
Oh! Where is the marker?
-It is under the chair.
Oh no! Where is the book?
-It is on the bookshelf.
I love my school bag!

Choose the correct answer

Where is the book?
❏ on the bag ❏ on the desk ❏ on the bookshelf

Where is the marker?
❏ on the desk ❏ on the bag ❏ under the chair

Where is the crayon?
❏ in the bag ❏ on the desk ❏ on the chair

Choose the correct picture

Where is the pencil?

Where is the notebook?

Where is the ruler?

Complete the reading with the words from the box below

My school bag is beautiful
The pencil is ___ the bag.
The pen is in the bag too.
The crayon is in the bag and the notebook is also in the bag.
Oops! Where is the _____?
-It is under the desk.
Oh! Where is the _____?
-It is _____the chair.
Oh no! Where is the _____?
-It is _____the bookshelf.
I love my school bag!

in • on • under • pen • pencil • crayon • ruler • sharpener
• eraser • book • notebook • marker • scissors

Write the words. Say them aloud.

pen   eraser

pencil   book

crayon   notebook

ruler   marker

sharpener   scissors

A pronoun is a word that takes the place of a noun. The pronouns **IT** takes the place of a singular *object*

The book is on the bookshelf.
It is on the bookshelf.

The prepositions ON, IN, UNDER, show the location of nouns.

The bag is on the chair

The bag is under the chair

The ruler is in the bag

Look at the pictures and write the missing words

Where is the sharpener?

-It is _____ the chair.

Where is the eraser?

-It is _____ the board.

Where is the book?

-It is _____ the bookshelf.

Complete the sentences

Where is the ruler?

-It is _____ the desk.

this   **on**   **table**

Where is the marker?

-_____ is on the chair.

the   **it**   **is**

Where is the book?
-It _____ on the bookshelf.

the   **this**   **is**

How well did you do in this unit?

⭐ ⭐ ⭐

_____

Write the CAN DO statement and assess yourself:

I can...

_____

_____

_____

_____

_____

MY ENGLISH ZONE

Learn the colors and shapes

Learning colors

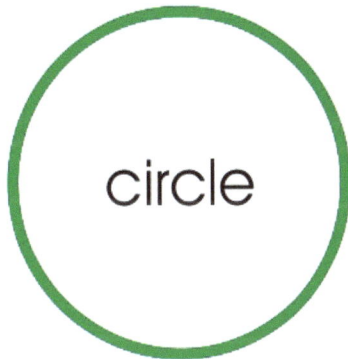

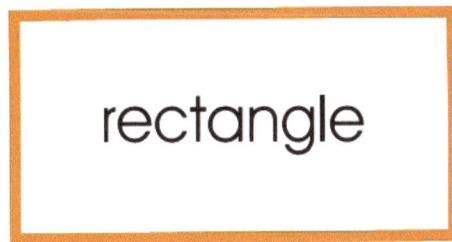

red

blue

yellow

green

orange

square

circle

triangle

oval

rectangle

Practice the dialogs

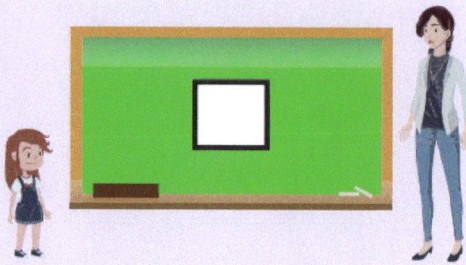

Is this a yellow square?
-No it isn't yellow square.
It's a green square.

Is this a green oval?
-No it isn't a green oval.
-It is a yellow oval.

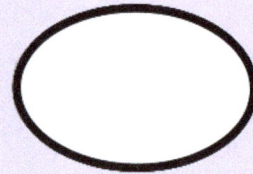

Is this a yellow rectangle?
-No, it isn't a yellow rectangle.
-It is an orange rectangle.

Is this a blue triangle?
-No, it isn't a blue triangle.
-It is a red triangle.

Now you!

Is this a/an _____ _____?
No, it isn't a/an _____ _____.
It is a/an _____ _____.

Colors and shapes

Miss Patty teaches us about colors and shapes today.
Now I know, this is isn't a red circle and it isn't a blue circle.
It is a yellow circle!
This isn't a red square and it isn't blue square. It is a green square!
This isn't a red rectangle and it isn't a blue rectangle.
It is an orange rectangle!
This isn't a blue triangle and it isn't a yellow triangle.
It is a red triangle!
This isn't a red oval and it isn't an orange oval. It is a blue oval!
What is your favorite color and shape?
I love colors and shapes!

Choose the correct answer

What color is the circle?

❏ red   ❏ blue   ❏ yellow

What color is the square?

❏ red ❏ green   ❏ blue

What color is the rectangle?

❏ orange   ❏ blue   ❏ red

What color is the triangle?

❏ blue   ❏ red   ❏ yellow

What color is the oval?

❏ blue   ❏ orange   ❏ red

Based on the reading answer true or false

1. It is a yellow circle.
   true ❏   false ❏

2. It is an orange square
   true ❏   false ❏

3. It is a red rectangle
   true ❏   false ❏

4. It is green triangle
   true ❏   false ❏

5. It is blue oval
   true ❏   false ❏

Complete the reading with the words from the box below

This is my school bag!
Miss Patty today teaches us about colors and shapes.

Now, I know this isn't a red (shape) _____
and it isn't a blue (shape)_____ . It is a yellow (shape)_____ !
This isn't a (color)_____ square
and it isn't (color)_____ square. It is a (color)_____ square!
This isn't a blue (shape)_____
and it isn't a yellow (shape)_____ . It is a red (shape)_____ !
This isn't a (color)_____ oval
and it isn't a (color)_____ oval. It is a (color)_____ oval!

What is your favorite color and shape?
I love colors and shapes!

red • yellow • green • blue • orange
square • circle • triangle • rectangle • oval

Write the words. Say them aloud.

red	orange	triangle
blue	square	oval
yellow	circle	
green	rectangle	

52

Adjectives are words that describe.
Colors describe nouns.
This is a **red** circle.
Adjectives are not used with plural form.

The negative form of the verb BE for the singular form: **Is+not.**
It can also be used in its contracted form: **isn't.**

We use a short negative answer:
No, (comma) **it isn't.** (period)

Choose the correct answer

1. Is this a yellow circle?
   Yes, it is.
   No, it isn't.
   No it is.
2. Is this a blue rectangle?
   No, it isn't.
   Yes, it is.
   No, it is.
3. Is this a red triangle?
   No, it is.
   Yes, it is.
   No, it isn't.
4. Is this an orange square?
   No it isn't
   No, it isn't.
   Yes, it is.

Order the sentences

1. This _____ a _____ _____.
   yellow   is   square

2. _____ is _____ a
   _____ triangle.
   red   this   not

3. It _____ a _____
   _____.
   rectangle   isn't   blue

4. _____ isn't _____
   orange _____.
   an   circle   it

5. _____ is _____ _____
   oval.

How well did you do in this unit?

Write the CAN DO statement and assess yourself:

I can...

Learn the family members

Sandy

father   mother   sister   brother   baby   grandfather   grandmother

Practice the dialogs

Who is this?
-This is my
mother.

Who is this?
-This is my
father.

Who is this?
-This is my
grandmother.

Who is this?
-This is my
grandfather.

Who is this?
-This is my
sister.

Who is this?
-This is my
brother.

Who is this?
-This is my
baby brother.

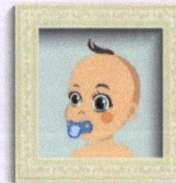

Now you!

Who is this/that?
This/that is my_____

This is my beautiful family

That is my father and this is my mother.
This is my brother and this is my sister.
That is my grandfather and that is my grandmother.
Oh yes! That is my baby brother.
I love my family!

Re-order the words

_ _ _ _ _ _
t e r h m o

_ _ _ _ _ _
e r h t a f

_ _ _ _ _ _
b o h r t e

_ _ _ _ _ _
s r i e s t

_ _ _ _
y a b b

_ _ _ _ _ _ _ _ _ _ _
r g e r h a t n a d f

Choose the correct family member

This is my mother
☐ ☐ ☐

This is my sister
☐ ☐ ☐

This is my father
☐ ☐ ☐

This is my baby brother
☐ ☐ ☐

Complete the reading with the words from the box below

This is my beautiful family!
This is my _____ and that is
my_____.
This is my _____ and that is my
_____.
This is my _____ and that is my
_____. Oh yes!
And that is my_____,

I love my family!

mother • father • grandmother • grandfather
brother • sister • baby brother

Write the words. Say them aloud.

brother	brother
father	father
grandfather	grandfather
grandmother	grandmother
mother	mother
sister	sister

Possessive adjectives are used to show possession of something.
My book= ownership

When we refer to people it refers to relationship.
My mother= relationship

The possessive adjective for the 1st person "I" is "**MY**"

"**Who**" asks for a person.
For example:
"**Who** is that?"
"That is my **mother**."

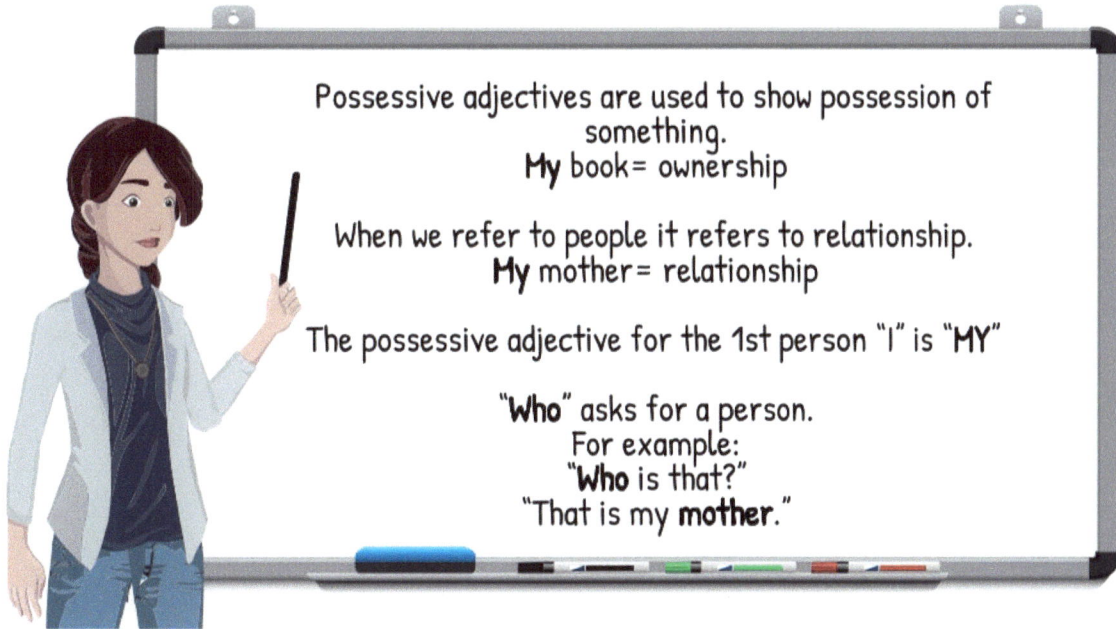

Write the correct sentence

____ ____ ____ _____.

____ ____ ____ _____.

____ ____ ____ _____.

____ ____ ____ _____.

____ ____ ____ _____.

Order the sentences

1. _____ _____ _____ ?

   is   Who   that

2. That _____ _____ _____ .

   father   my   is

3. ____ ____ my _____ .

   is   sister   this

4. ____ is ____ ?

   Who   that

5. ____ ____ ____

   grandmother.

   This   my   is

This is my grandfather.
This is my father.
This is my grandmother.
This is my sister.
This is my mother.

How well did you do in this unit?

Write the CAN DO statement and assess yourself:

I can...

Learn the rooms in the home

bedroom

bathroom

yard

living room

dining room

kitchen

Practice the dialogs

Is this the kitchen?
-No, it isn't. It's the dining room.

Is this the bedroom?
-No, it isn't. It's the living room.

Is this the dining room?
-No, it isn't. It's the kitchen.

Is this the bathroom?
-No, it isn't. It's the bedroom.

Now you!

Is this the _____?
No, it isn't. It's the
_____.

Welcome to my home!

This is the kitchen, it is a yellow kitchen.
This is the bedroom, it is a blue bedroom.
This is the bathroom, it is a green bathroom.
This is the living room; it is a red living room.
This is the yard. It is many colors.
I love my home!

Re-order the sentences

_____ _____ _____ green.
The   is   bathroom

_____ _____ the _____ .
This   yard   is

That ____ ____ _____ .
is   the   kitchen

____ _____ is ____ .
blue   the   bedroom.

Choose the correct color

The kitchen is:
❑ green ❑ yellow ❑ blue

The bedroom is:
❑ red ❑ blue ❑ orange

The bathroom is:
❑ blue ❑ orange ❑ green

The living room is:
❑ red ❑ orange ❑ yellow

Complete the reading with the words from the box below

Welcome to my home

This is the kitchen, it is a _____ (color) kitchen.

This is the yard, it is a _____ (color) yard.

This is the bedroom, it is a _____ (color) bedroom.

This is the living room, it is a _____ (color) living room.

I love my home!

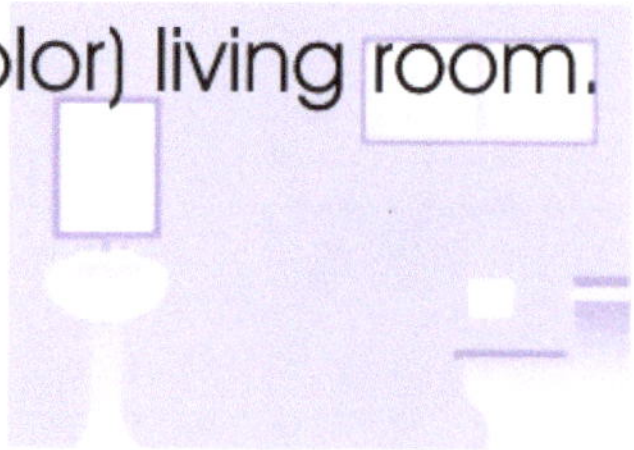

red • blue • yellow • orange • green

Write the words. Say them aloud.

kitchen   living room
bathroom   yard
bedroom   dining room

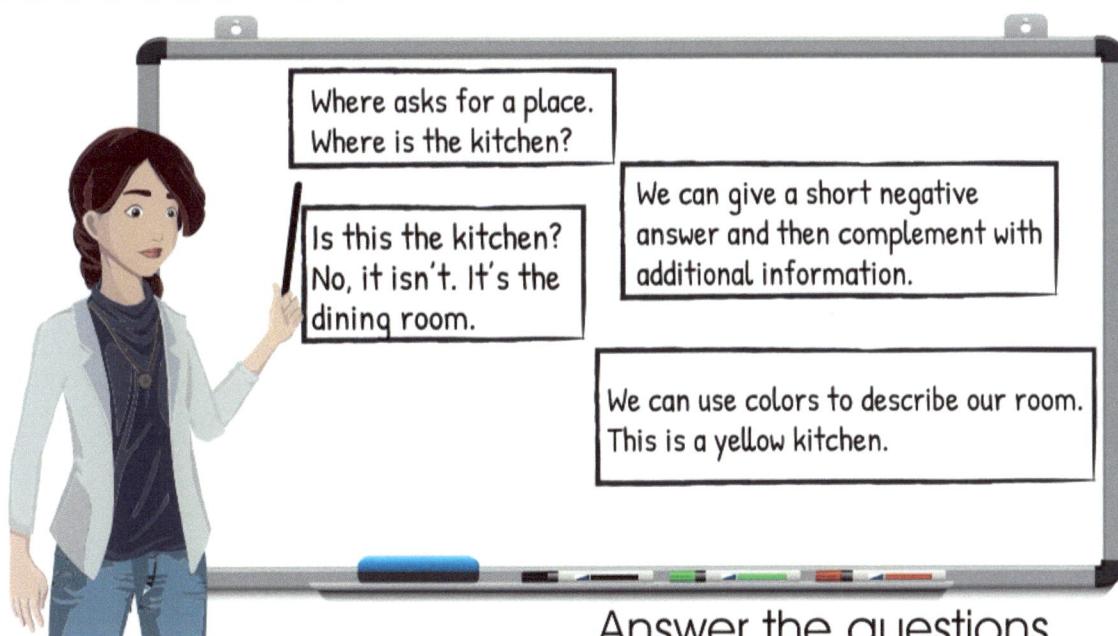

Where asks for a place.
Where is the kitchen?

Is this the kitchen?
No, it isn't. It's the dining room.

We can give a short negative answer and then complement with additional information.

We can use colors to describe our room. This is a yellow kitchen.

Answer the questions

Is this the bedroom?
-No, it isn't.
-It's the _____.

Is this the bathroom?
-No, it isn't.
-It's the _____.

Is this the dining room?
-No, it isn't.
-It's the _____.

Is this the kitchen?
-No, it isn't.
-It's the _____.

Is this the dining room?
-No, it isn't.
-It's the _____.

Complete the sentences

Is this a yellow kitchen?
-No, _____ isn't.
-It's a green _____.

Is this a green bathroom?
-No, it _____.
-It's a _____ bathroom.

Where _____ the dining room?

_____ is the yard?

Where is the _____?

bedroom • where
is • it • blue • isn't

How well did you do in this unit?

Write the CAN DO statement and assess yourself:

I can...

Learn the family and the rooms in the home

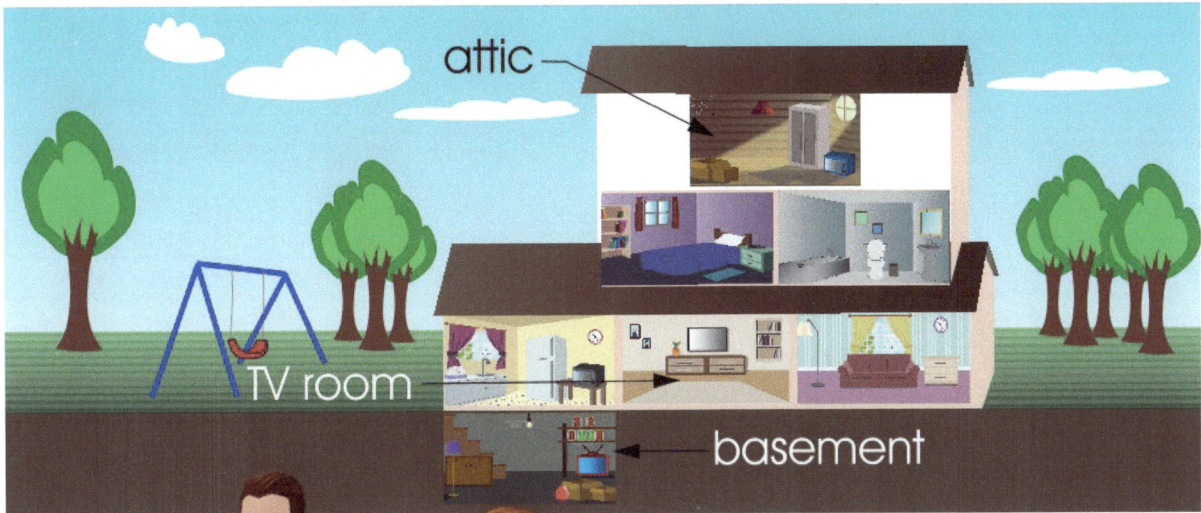

| uncle | aunt | cousin | cousin |

Practice the dialogs

Where is uncle?
-He is in the TV room.

Where is aunt?
-She is in bedroom.

Where is aunt?
-She is in the attic.

Where is cousin Tim?
-He is in the kitchen.

Where is cousin Mary?
-She is in the basement.

Where is mother?
-She is in the bedroom.

Where is grandmother?
-She is in the living room.

Now you!

Where is _____?
-He/she is in the
_____.

This is my family's home!

My father is in the TV room and
my mother is in the attic.
My cousin Mary is in the basement and
my brother is in the kitchen.
My aunt is in the bedroom and
uncle is in the living room.
Oh! Where is grandmother?
She is in the yard!.
I love my family's home!

Answer the questions

Where is grandmother?
❏ TV room ❏ attic ❏ yard

Where is uncle?
❏ bedroom ❏ basement
❏ living room

Where is aunt?
❏ bedroom ❏ kitchen ❏ yard

Where is brother?
❏ attic ❏ TV room ❏ kitchen

Where is cousin Mary?
❏ kitchen ❏ yard ❏ basement

Answer the questions

Is father in the yard?
-No, he isn't. He's in the

_____.

Is uncle in the bathroom?
-No, he isn't. He's in the

_____.

Is aunt in the dining room?
No, she isn't. She's in the

_____.

Complete the reading with the words from the box below

This is my family's home!

My _____ is in the _____ and my
_____ is in the _____ .

My _____ is in the _____ and my
_____ is in the _____ .

My _____ is in the _____ and my
_____ is in the _____ .

I love my family's home!

uncle • aunt • cousin • mother • father • grandmother
grandfather • brother • sister • kitchen • living room
dining room • bathroom • bedroom • basement • attic
yard • TV room

Write the words. Say them aloud.

uncle	bedroom	living room
aunt	kitchen	bathroom
cousin	basement	
attic	TV room	

Personal pronouns take the place of nouns.

He takes the place of male nouns
She takes the place of female nouns
It takes the place of things

My **father** is in the kitchen.
He is in the kitchen.
My **mother** is in the bathroom.
She is in the bathroom
The **bedroom** is blue.
It is blue.

Write the correct pronoun

(Mother)
_____ is in the attic.

(Father)
_____ is in the kitchen.

(The bedroom)
_____ is blue.

(Uncle Tim)
_____ is in the bathroom.

(Cousin Mary)
_____ is in the dining room.

(The kitchen)
_____ is yellow.

Choose the correct pronoun

<u>Father</u> is in the TV room.
❏ He   ❏ She   ❏ It

<u>The living room</u> is red.
❏ He   ❏ She   ❏ It

<u>Mother</u> is in the attic.
❏ He   ❏ She   ❏ It

<u>Cousin Mary</u> is in the basement.
❏ He   ❏ She   ❏ It

<u>Brother</u> is in the kitchen.
❏ He   ❏ She   ❏ It

<u>The kitchen</u> is yellow.
❏ He   ❏ She   ❏ It

How well did you do in this unit?

Write the CAN DO statement and assess yourself:

I can...

Learn the emotions

angry	happy	hungry	nervous
sad	scared	silly	sleepy
	thirsty	tired	

Find the emotions

L	N	L	W	X	G	I	J	I	I
C	D	T	S	Y	R	G	N	A	Y
N	E	H	I	R	Y	N	Z	O	P
N	R	I	L	G	P	E	Z	V	E
D	I	R	L	N	P	R	O	V	E
E	T	S	Y	U	A	V	R	H	L
R	T	T	R	H	H	O	D	A	S
A	U	Y	Y	R	H	U	P	X	V
C	N	I	C	O	Z	S	F	G	A
S	H	V	X	P	A	U	Y	O	S

ANGRY
HAPPY
HUNGRY
NERVOUS
SAD
SCARED
SILLY
SLEEPY
THIRSTY
TIRED

12.2

Practice the dialogs

Is father sad?
-No, he isn't. He's happy.

Is grandmother sleepy?
-No, she isn't. She's sad.

Is sister angry?
-No, she isn't. She's scared.

Is uncle hungry?
-No, he isn't. He's thirsty.

Is mother angry?
-No, she isn't. She's nervous.

Is aunt sleepy?
-No, she isn't. She's hungry

Is brother silly?
-No, he isn't. He's tired.

Now you!

Is _____ _____?
-No, he/she isn't.
He/she is _____.

How is your family today?

My father is sleepy today.
My mother is tired today.
My sister is thirsty today.
My brother is silly today.
My uncle is angry today.
My aunt is hungry today.
I love my family,
I am very happy today!

Match the questions with the correct emotion

- How is father today?
- How is mother today?
- How is sister today?
- How is brother today?
- How is uncle today?

Answer the questions

1. How is father today?
   ☐ happy ☐ sleepy ☐ hungry

2. How is mother today?
   ☐ happy ☐ tired ☐ angry

3. How is sister today?
   ☐ thirsty ☐ sad ☐ sleepy

4. How is brother today?
   ☐ silly ☐ angry ☐ happy

5. How is uncle today?
   ☐ thirsty ☐ tired ☐ angry

Complete the reading with the words from the box below

How is your family today?

My father is _____ today.
My mother is _____ today.
My brother is _____ today.
My sister is _____ today.
My grandmother is _____ today.
And I am very _____ today.
I love my family!

angry • happy • hungry • nervous • sad
scared • silly • sleepy • thirsty • tired

Write the words. Say them aloud.

angry	scared
happy	silly
hungry	sleepy
nervous	thirsty
sad	tired

Wh- questions request information.

Who asks for a person.
Who is that?

Where asks for a place.
Where is mother?

What asks for thing or an action.
What is that?

How asks for a number or the way you feel.
How are you today?

Complete the questions with the correct Wh-question

Who • What • Where
What • How

_____ is your mother?
She's happy.

_____ is this?
It's a book.

_____ is your sister?
Nancy is my sister.

_____ is your father?
He's in the kitchen

_____ are you today?
I'm tired.

_____ is the pencil?
It's under the chair.

Choose the correct pronoun

Father is in the TV room.
❑ He ❑ She ❑ It

The living room is red.
❑ He ❑ She ❑ It

Mother is in the attic.
❑ He ❑ She ❑ It

Cousin Mary is in the basement.
❑ He ❑ She ❑ It

Brother is in the kitchen.
❑ He ❑ She ❑ It

The kitchen is yellow.
❑ He ❑ She ❑ It

How well did you do in this unit?

Write the CAN DO statement and assess yourself:

I can...

Learn the clothes

blouse

skirt

shirt

dress

blouses

skirts

shirts

dresses

jeans

pants

shoes

tennis shoes

Find the clothes

S	S	E	A	N	Y	P	C	X	I	J	I
V	E	H	E	B	Q	A	M	O	E	C	C
O	S	S	O	H	J	N	I	A	E	W	S
X	U	J	S	E	I	T	N	Z	A	T	S
N	O	A	I	E	S	S	H	I	R	T	S
T	L	O	I	H	R	N	R	I	C	W	I
U	B	J	N	E	C	D	K	H	K	X	Z
P	U	B	Z	M	T	S	P	E	M	F	F
U	U	B	L	Y	W	P	R	T	B	J	T
T	R	X	F	J	G	E	R	T	D	S	M
S	E	O	H	S	S	I	N	N	E	T	W
D	T	Q	Y	P	T	W	V	P	X	A	Z

DRESSES

SKIRTS

BLOUSES

SHOES

SHIRTS

PANTS

JEANS

TENNIS SHOES

Practice the dialogs

Look! Those are my skirts.
-Are they green skirts?
No, they aren't.
They are red skirts.

Look! These are my jeans!
-Are they red jeans?
No, they aren't.
They are blue jeans.

Look! Those are my shirts!
-Are they blue shirts?
No, they aren't.
They are yellow shirts.

Look! These are my dresses.
-Are they red dresses?
No, they aren't.
They are orange dresses.

Look! Those are my blouses.
-Are they orange blouses?
No, they aren't.
They are green blouses.

Look! These are my pants.
-Are they blue pants?
No, they aren't.
They are green pants.

Look! Those are my shoes.
-Are they red shoes?
No, they aren't.
They are blue shoes.

Now you!

Look! These/those are my _____.
Are they _____ _____.
No, they aren't. They are _____ _____.

These are my favorite clothes!

These are my favorite clothes!
They are not blue blouses and they are not yellow skirts.
They are red dresses.
I love my red dresses!

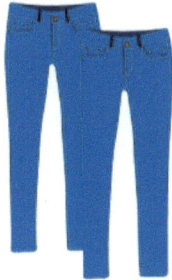

These are my favorite clothes!
They are not orange shirts and they are not green pants.
They are blue jeans.
I love my blue jeans!

Complete the sentences

They _____ red dresses.

❑ is ❑ are ❑ am

They are _____ blue skirts.

❑ am ❑ is ❑ not

_____ are orange blouses.

❑ those ❑ it ❑ you

These are yellow _____.

❑ shirt ❑ blue ❑ shirts

_____ are not green pants.

❑ it ❑ she ❑ those

Answer the questions

What are Sandy's favorite clothes?
Are they blue blouses?
❑ Yes ❑ No
Are they yellow skirts?
❑ Yes ❑ No
Are they red dresses?
❑ Yes ❑ No
What are Andy's favorite clothes?
Are they orange shirts?
❑ Yes ❑ No
Are they green pants?
❑ Yes ❑ No
Are they blue jeans?
❑ Yes ❑ No

Complete the reading with the words from the box below

At my favorite store

These are my favorite clothes!
These are my favorite clothes!
They are not _____ _____ and
they are not _____ _____.
They are _____ _____.
I love my _____ _____!

dresses	shirts	red
skirts	pants	yellow
blouses	jeans	green
shoes	tennis shoes	blue
		orange

Write the words. Say them aloud.

dresses   pants
skirts   jeans
blouses   tennis
shoes
shirts   shoes

Plural Demonstrative Pronouns

We use **THESE** to talk about people or things near us.
We use **THAT** to talk about people or things far from us.

We form the plural by adding "**S**" to noun.
Skirt (singular) skirt+**s** =skirts (plural)

They is the personal pronoun for plurals.
The skirts are green.
They are green.

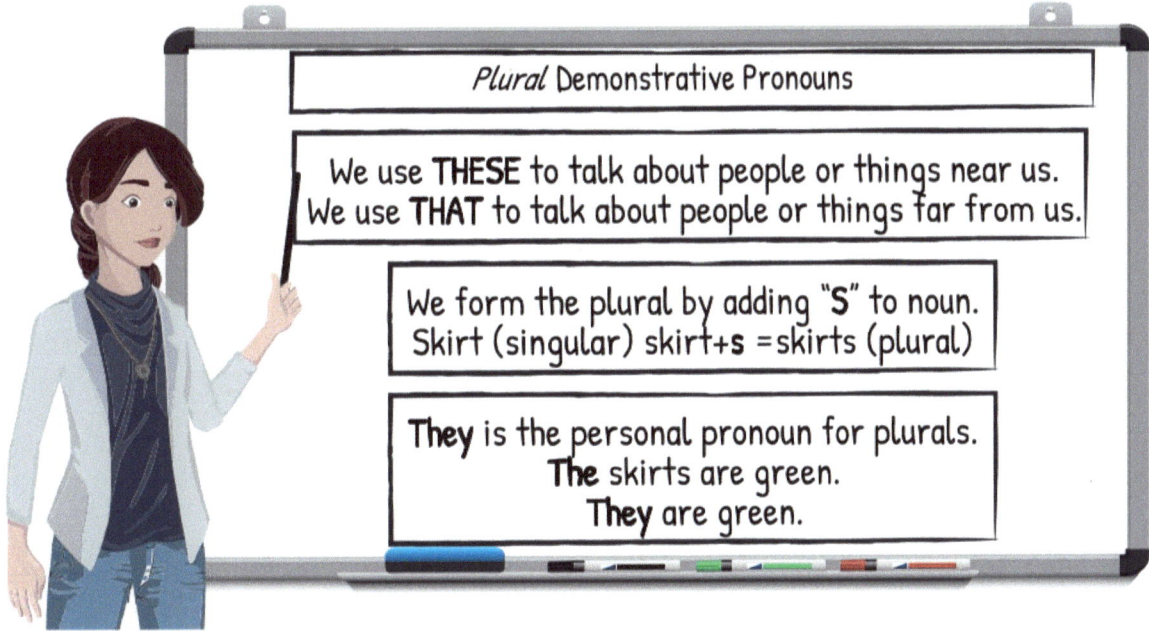

Re-order the sentences

1. _____ _____ _____ _____ .
   socks   they   green   are

2. _____ _____ _____ _____ .
   jeans   aren't   blue   these

3. _____ _____ _____ _____ .
   are   orange   blouses   those

4. _____ _____ _____ _____ .
   are   they   pants   orange

5. _____ _____ _____ _____ .
   yellow   shirts   are   they

Choose the correct word to complete the sentence

They are green _____.
☐ sock ☐ socks

_____ are blue skirts.
☐ It ☐ They

Those _____ red shoes.
☐ is ☐ are

_____ are yellow jeans.
☐ These ☐ This

_____ are orange dresses.
☐ Those ☐ That

How well did you do in this unit?

Write the CAN DO statement and assess yourself:

I can...

Describe the clothes

brown

skirt

white

blouse

pink

pants

black

tennis shoes

purple

shoes

Practice the dialogs

Excuse me! Is there a pink blouse?
-No, there isn't.
-But there is a white blouse.
Oh, no! Thank you.
-You're welcome.

Excuse me! Is there a white pair of tennis shoes?
-No, there isn't.
-But there is a black pair of tennis shoes.
Oh, no! Thank you.
-You're welcome.

Excuse me! Is there a purple skirt?
-No, there isn't.
-But there is a brown skirt.
Oh, no! Thank you.
-You're welcome.

Excuse me! Is there a black pair of shoes?
-No, there isn't.
-But there is a purple pair of shoes.
Oh, no! Thank you.
-You're welcome.

Now you!

Excuse me!
Is there a _____ ?
-No, there isn't.
-But there is a _____ .
Oh, no! Thank you.
-You're welcome.

This is my favorite store!

There are beautiful blouses here.
There are purple blouses; red blouses,
and my favorite: WHITE blouses!
There are also elegant shoes here.
There are white shoes; there are black shoes,
and my favorite: PURPLE shoes!
There are also new pants here.
There are brown pants; there are white pants,
and my favorite: PINK pants!
And there are beautiful skirts here.
There are purple skirts, there are white skirts,
and my favorite: BROWN skirts!
For sure, this is my favorite store!

Answer the questions

Are there brown shoes?
No, there aren't. But there are

_____.

Are there black blouses?
No, there aren't. But there are

_____.

Are there purple pants?
No, there aren't. But there are

_____.

Are there black skirts?
No, there aren't. But there are

_____.

What is there in my favorite store?

There are:
- ☐ purple blouses
- ☐ green blouses
- ☐ orange blouses

My favorite blouse is:
- ☐ pink blouse
- ☐ white blouse
- ☐ purple blouse

There are:
- ☐ blue shoes
- ☐ black shoes
- ☐ red shoes

Favorite shoes are:
- ☐ white shoes
- ☐ red shoes
- ☐ purple shoes

Complete the reading with the words from the box below

This is my favorite store!

There are beautiful blouses here.

There are _____ blouses; _____ blouses, and my favorite: _____ blouses!

There are also elegant shoes here.

There are _____ shoes; there are _____ shoes, and my favorite: _____ shoes!

There are also new pants here.

There are _____ pants; there are _____ pants, and my favorite: _____ pants!

And there are beautiful skirts here.

There are _____ skirts, there are _____ skirts, and my favorite: _____ skirts!

For sure, this is my favorite store!

pink • white • black • brown • purple

Write the words. Say them aloud.

pink   blouse

white   skirt

black   shoes

brown   pants

purple

THERE IS / THERE ARE
It means that something exists (or doesn't exist)

The *questions* for is:
Is there a green dress?
Are there red shoes?

There is, is used for singular
There is a green dress.
There are, is used for plurals
There are red shoes.

The *negative* form is:
There isn't (is not) a green dress.
There aren't (are not) red shoes.

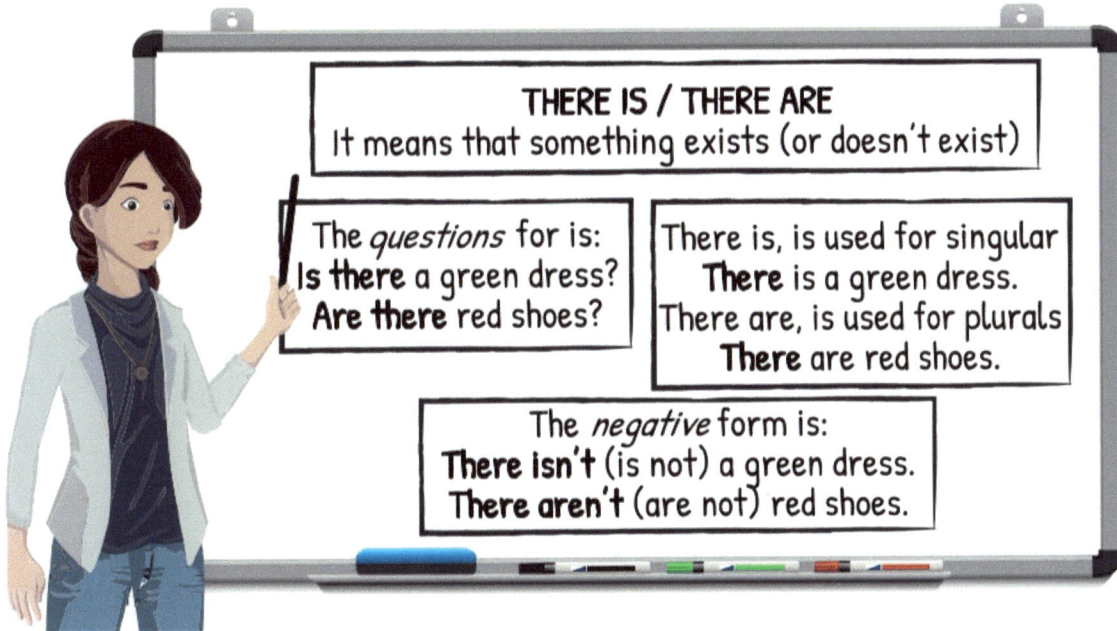

Re-order the sentences

___ ___ ___ ___ ___ .

shirt red a is there

___ ___ ___ ___ .

are there shoes black

___ ___ ___ ___ ___ .

blouse yellow isn't there a

___ ___ ___ ___ .

There pants brown aren't

___ ___ ___ ___ ___ ___ .

an orange there is skirt ?

___ ___ ___ ___ ___ .

socks green there are ?

Choose the correct word to complete the sentence

There _____ a white dress.
• is • are
There _____ white pants.
• is • are
There are _____ shirts.
• reds • red
There is a _____ skirt.
• reds • red
_____ there yellow socks?
• is • are
_____ there a yellow blouse?
• is • are
There _____ a blue shoe.
• isn't • aren't
There _____ blue jeans.
• isn't • aren't

How well did you do in this unit?

Write the CAN DO statement and assess yourself:

I can...

Describe the clothes

comfortable

jacket

nice

shorts

big

sweater

small

T-shirt

Practice the dialogs

Excuse me! How much is the sweater?
-It's $ 10.00 Dlls. It's very nice!
Yes, it's very nice. Thank you.
-You're welcome.

$10.00

Excuse me! How much is the T-shirt?
-It's $5.00 Dlls. It's very big!
Yes, it's very big! Thank you.
-You're welcome.

$5.00

Excuse me! How much is the jacket?
-It's $20.00 Dlls. It's very comfortable!
Yes, it's very comfortable! Thank you.
-You're welcome.

$20.00

Excuse me! How much are the shorts?
-They're $10.00 Dlls. They're very small.
Yes, they're very small! Thank you.
-You're welcome.

$10.00

Now you!

Excuse me! How much is the _____?
It's $_____ Dlls. It's very _____!
Yes, it's very _____! Thank you.
You're welcome.

At my favorite shop!

The prices at my favorite shop are very low!
The big sweater is only $18.00 and the yellow sweater is $15.00.
The small T-shirt is $3.00 and the red T-shirt $5.00.
The blue jacket is $20.00 and the comfortable jacket is $17.00.
The brown shorts are $10.00 and the nice shorts are $9.00.
Yes, the prices at my favorite shop are very low!

Answer the questions

Example:
How much is the blue jacket?
The blue jacket is $20.00 Dlls.

How much is the red T-shirt?
_____.

How much is the yellow sweater?
_____.

How much are the brown shorts?
_____.

How much is the big sweater?
_____.

How much is the small T-shirt?
_____.

What are the prices?
Match the sentences with the price

The comfortable jacket is seventeen dollars.	$10.00
The yellow sweater is fifteen dollars.	$5.00
The big sweater is eighteen dollars.	$17.00
The brown shorts are ten dollars.	$15.00
The red T-shirt is five dollars.	$18.00

Complete the reading with the following words. You may write them in any order you wish.

At my favorite shop!

The prices at my favorite shop are very low!
The big sweater is only $ _____
and the yellow sweater is $ _____ .
The small T-shirt is $ _____
and the red T-shirt $ _____ .
The _____ _____ is $ 20.00
and the _____ _____ is $ 17.00.
The _____ _____ are $ 10.00
and the _____ _____ are $ 9.00.
Yes, the prices at my favorite shop are very low!

jacket • blue • comfortable • shorts • red • nice
t-shirt • brown • big • sweater • yellow • small
5.00 • 15.00 • 9.00 • 18.00 • 7.00 • 17.00
10.00 • 20.00

Write the words. Say them aloud.

jacket   comfortable
shorts   nice
T-shirt   big
sweater   small

We use **how much** to ask for prices.

How much is the jacket?
How much are the shorts?

The jacket (IT) is $10.00 Dlls.
The shorts (THEY) are $9.00 Dlls.

Find the words

```
R  E  T  A  E  W  S  X  I  T
D  S  O  T  H  W  L  B  S  Q
M  E  R  B  W  O  H  H  L  G
O  I  I  A  T  Y  I  M  W  P
V  G  C  R  L  R  Q  U  T  R
N  I  O  N  T  L  E  C  E  P
N  H  M  U  I  W  O  H  K  L
S  M  A  L  L  C  P  D  C  C
J  E  C  R  U  T  E  A  A  D
W  K  R  K  J  B  L  G  J  S
```

JACKET	SHORT	T-SHIRT
SWEATER	COMFORTABLE	NICE
BIG	SMALL	DOLLARS
HOW	MUCH	

Write the correct price

Example:
The blue jacket is $20.00 Dlls.
It's twenty dollars.

The comfortable jacket is
$17.00 Dlls.
_____.

The yellow sweater is
$15.00 Dlls.
_____.

The big sweater is
$18.00 Dlls.
_____.

The brown shorts are
$10.00 Dlls.
_____.

The nice shorts are
$9.00 Dlls.
_____.

How well did you do in this unit?

_____

Write the CAN DO statement and assess yourself:

I can...

REFERENCES

• Communicative Language Learning. Retrieved August 23, 2019 from:
http://www.educationbridge-id.com/news-a-article/72-communicative-language-teaching-clt.html
• Brown, H. Douglas (1994). Principles of Language Learning and Teaching. Prentice Hall.
• Beale, Jason (2008). Is communicative language teaching a thing of the past?. TESOL article.
• Harmer, Jeremy (2007). How to teach English. Pearson Longman.
• Richards, Jack C (2002). Methodology in Language Teaching. Cambridge University Press.
• Willis, Jane (1996). A Framework for Task-Based Learning. Longman.
• Hermitt, A. (2015). Spiral Learning, a superior approach? In Families.com. Retrieved January 9th, 2015, from http://www.families.com/blog/spiral-learning-a-superior approach.
• Fleming, N. Baume, D. (2006) Learning Styles.
• Again: VARKing up the right tree! , Educational Developments, SEDA Ltd, Issue 7.4 Nov. 2006.
• Harmer, Jeremy. How to Teach English. Harlow: Longman, 1998. Krashen, Stephen D., and Terrell, Tracy D. The Natural Approach. Oxford: Pergamon, 1983.
• Sökmen, Anita J. "Current Trends in Teaching Second Language Vocabulary". In Vocabulary: *Description, Acq*uisition and Pedagogy, edited by N. Schmitt and M. McCarthy, 237-257 England: Cambridge University Press, 1997.
• Snow, Marguerite Ann. "T*eaching English as a Second or Foreign Language". In* Content-Based and Immersion Models for Second and Foreign Language Teaching" Edited by M. Celce-Murcia. Heinle & Heinle Thomson Learning, 2001.
• Roth, Genevieve. Tea*ching Very Young Children. Ric*hmond Handbooks for English Teachers. London: Richmond Publishing. 1998.

ABOUT THE AUTHOR

Patricia Avila has been an English teacher for more than 45 years in her native Tijuana, B. C. She has a Bachelor's in Education from the National Pedagogical University (UPN).

Her experience as a teacher ranges from Kindergarten to Masters. She has functioned as coordinator of Bachelor's in ESL Teaching, as well as for various other universities; she has also worked as an Academic Consultant for different Publishing Houses for more than 15 years. Her wide experience and love for young learners has given her the opportunity to share with you **MY ENGLISH ZONE THE BOOK**, a series that will enhance the learning of English in a dynamic and fun way.